HALLOWEEN NIGHT
13 SCARY TALES OF TERROR
BOOK 4

HALLOWEEN NIGHT

13 SCARY TALES OF TERROR
BOOK 4

REYNA YOUNG

Printed in the United States of America.

For more information, or to book an event, contact :
Email: kcl3rc@yahoo.com
www.lastdoorwayproductions.com

Back Cover Image: Jason Dube
Back Colors Andy Tiu
Cover Design by Reyna and John Gillette

ISBN – Paperback: 979-8-8691-7527-4

First Edition: July 2023
10 9 8 7 6 5 4 3 2 1

More books by Reyna Young:

Also Available on eBook

1. Creature of Stowe Cabin
2. Hanover Falls
3. Horror Lullabies
4. Mr. Torture
5. Once upon a Horror
6. Nevermore Books
7. The Christmas Creature
8. Hamsterstein
9. Bride of Hamsterstein
10. Halloween Zombie Party
11. The Werewolf of Wolf Lake
12. The Mummy Awakened on Mummy Street
13. Hanover Falls Part Two
Monsters Unleashed: There's a Human Under my Bed
Monsters Unleashed: Mommy Monster

The Pumpkin Man of Hallow Falls
(Picture Book)

Halloween Night: 13 Scary Tales of Terror Book One
Halloween Night: 13 Scary Tales of Terror Book Two
Halloween Night: 13 Scary Tales of Terror Book Three

DEDICATED TO LOGAN
(MY LITTLE BOO)

You're Back For More Spooky Surprises...

I can hardly fathom your return; I sensed your relentless yearning for another serving of spine-chilling tales within the confines of my eerie library.

Pay no attention to Stan lurking there, his insatiable hunger prevails yet rest assured, he won't devour you; he has grown to appreciate your presence, I believe.

But let me caution you about our latest addition, Blacky, a pesky bat with an insidious penchant for playing wicked pranks on unsuspecting souls.

Now, without further ado, select a book, any book, that's right. Sink into the comfort of this worn armchair, adorned with overgrown cobwebs, yet still inviting.

There you go, release a deep breath, and brace yourself to delve into a book that shall send shivers down your spine, or dare I say, compel you to read more...

It followed me home

Marcus released a weary exhale, his tired eyes desperately yearning to stop reading. After an entire day of study at the library, he longed to bid farewell to his homework and go home.

Collecting his things, he walked outside to see his friends, their animated conversation filling the night air. His intention was to say goodbye and leave, yet a sinister tale, being told by his friend Jane, caught his attention.

Eagerly, she recounted the chilling chronicle of a creature lurking within the shadows of the town, relentlessly tormenting its unsuspecting prey by trailing them home and scraping its claws along their very doors to mark their doom.

Marcus found himself overtaken by uncontrollable laughter; his friend thought he was being immature not to believe her. She spun a spine-chilling tale to him, recounting the dreadful vanishing of several kids that her parents knew in school back in the day, for they disappeared without a trace, swallowed by the night as they foolishly ventured home alone.

With an uncanny knack for preying on its victims, this ghastly creature had but one goal—to transform the unfortunate souls into its own kind.

Marcus shook his head in disbelief and rolled his eyes at the story spun by his friend. He was convinced she was merely playing a wicked prank on him. Determined to prove them wrong, he walked alone instead of walking home in a group.

Marcus walked home in the dark, the wind howling like a banshee on the prowl. Still laughing at his friend Jane's wild tales, he couldn't shake the lingering sense of unease.

He had stayed out later than usual when he likes to be home before dark, but a creature lurking in the shadows? She had to be trying to get his skin to crawl.

Lost in his thoughts, Marcus marched on, his earphones plugged in, drowning out the whispers of the night. Yet, as he walked on, a sinister presence slithered into his consciousness. A chill ran down his spine. He couldn't shake the uncanny feeling that his eyes were fixed upon him.

Marcus spun around, scanning the emptiness encircling him. No one. Just an empty street. Swallowing his fear and amplifying his paranoia, he couldn't shake the feeling of being watched.

Panic overcame him, and Marcus increased his pace. His heart pounded like a drum in his chest, his breaths shallow and frantic.

He couldn't shake off the unsettling feeling that his friend's tale had gotten to him. Plowing ahead, he carried on with his walk, but suddenly, a blood-curdling shriek pierced his ears, causing him to startle and leap into the air. Something swiftly dashed past him, causing him to spin around in sheer panic. Without hesitation, he sprinted home, praying that whatever it was wouldn't catch up to him.

Anxiety gripped him tightly as he fidgeted in his pocket, fumbling for his keys, eager to unlock the safety of his home. As his mother approached, she casually informed him that dinner awaited him at the dining table. Glancing out the window, his heart seized his chest; he felt better behind closed doors.

The following morning, he stepped outside, only to discover scratch marks etched onto his door.

The horrifying thought of his friend's story lingered persistently in his mind.

It followed him home...

Mishipeshu – The Water Monster

Delilah giddily hatched a plan to hang out with her pals, Sam and Claire. She had a secret spot in mind - a lake surrounded by forbidding signs that warned against stepping foot in its murky waters.

Despite Claire's apprehension, Delilah saw it as the perfect spot for some fun. However, a cloud of hesitation shadowed Claire's mood. She didn't like the idea of getting caught and hauled off to jail, nor did she dismiss the significance of those signs all around.

DO NOT SWIM
IN THE LAKE

On the other hand, Sam jumped at the opportunity to do something bad.

Looking at the lake, Delilah couldn't contain her excitement any longer. She quickly shed her shoes, pants, and hat, ready to plunge into the mysterious depths.

Sam followed suit by removing his footwear, feeding off Delilah's excitement.

Claire, however, stood her ground with folded arms, irritated about their presence there. Voicing her concern, Claire called out, "It's really not a good idea, you guys."

Delilah jeered back, "You're such a buzzkill, Claire."

"Yeah, a total buzzkill!" Sam echoed, copying Delilah.

As Claire slowly inched away from the shimmering water, a sudden rustling from behind sent a chill down her spine. With a quick spin, she caught sight of a figure lurking among the gnarled trees, his piercing gaze fixed upon her. A blood-curdling scream escaped her lips, alerting both Sam and Delilah before they could jump into the water.

Emerging from the shadows, the man approached cautiously. "Hey! What do you think you're doing?"

Sam bellowed, his voice laced with concern. "Stay away from her!"

Raising his hands in a gesture of surrender, the man spoke, "I mean you no harm. I had to warn you, you mustn't venture into those waters. The signs are there for a reason."

Sam and Delilah exchanged amused glances, chuckling at the man's warning.

"Oh, please," Delilah scoffed. "We'll be just fine."

There was a scared look in Claire's eyes as she turned to Delilah. "Perhaps we should listen," she pleaded. "It's not worth the risk."

But Delilah, stubborn as ever, ignored Claire's plea and proceeded to dip her foot into the water.

In a desperate cry, Claire shouted, "No!" Yet her words fell upon deaf ears as Sam and Delilah jumped in the water without a care in the world.

"See? Nothing to worry about!" Sam shrugged.

Claire asked the old man, "What's wrong with this water?"

Sadness darkened the man's features as he began his chilling tale. "This lake is cursed, cursed for centuries. Native American tribes speak of a malevolent creature haunting these waters—an abominable fusion of dragon and feline if you can believe it."

"Absurd!" Delilah yelled out with a dismissive snort. "Sounds like a mere myth."

The old man's eyes bore into Delilah's. "It may sound like a myth, but these waters have claimed countless lives. I've witnessed it first-hand."

Suddenly, Sam's playful demeanor vanished, replaced with a look of sheer terror. Delilah asked him what was wrong, but before he could utter a word, an invisible force yanked him beneath the surface, leaving Delilah to shriek in horror.

"It's here," the old man muttered, his voice barely a whisper. Trembling with fear,

Claire grasped the man's arm. "What's here?"

Delilah kicked her legs with all her might, propelling herself towards the safety of the shore, desperately calling for Claire. Full of panic, Claire sprinted to the water's edge, stretching her hand out towards Delilah. "Hurry, grab my hand!" she yelled.

Delilah's heart raced as she swam with all her strength, determined to reach her friend. But to her horror, something monstrous leaped out of the water, snatching Claire and pulling her beneath the surface. Delilah's scream tore through the air as she thrashed in the water, her determination to try to escape the lake overwhelming her fear.

She had to make it to land and had to find help. But fate was cruel, as something sinister seized her ankle, yanking her back into the depths, dragging her around, and finally pulling her down into the abyss, never resurfacing again.

The weathered old man stood nearby, his face etched with sorrow. "I warned them," he mumbled quietly, his voice carrying a sense of regret. He turned away and walked off, "That's why there are signs, and they never listen, these kids. They never listen."

The Whistling Man

Sofia awoke abruptly, her senses heightened by a strange, eerie noise echoing throughout the house.

She squinted her eyes, scanning the darkness of her room. Urgently, she thrust herself out of bed, determined to investigate the source of the noise.

With delicate caution, she opened her bedroom door, the hinges letting out a menacing squeak that seemed to pierce the silence. Almost in response, the noise downstairs ceased, sending a shiver down Sofia's spine.

Summoning her courage, Sofia ventured into the dimly lit hallway, her steps muffled by the threadbare carpet. But just as she reached the top of the stairs, the sound resumed its haunting presence. Suddenly, a hand clamped firmly over her mouth, muffling any potential scream. It was her Abuela, pulling her back and whisking her into the safety of her bedroom, shutting the door gently behind them.

Confused and afraid, Sofia whispered to her abuela, her voice barely audible, "What is happening? What's wrong?"

"Don't go downstairs, Sofia," her abuela warned, the words dripping with unspoken terror. "There is someone down there. Someone you should never meet. I-I'm waiting for them to leave."

Sofia's mind swirled with a whirlwind of questions. "I don't understand... Who is it? Why are they here?"

Her abuela placed a comforting hand on her shoulder, trying to calm her trembling granddaughter. "Don't you worry; it's going to be alright. Just stay in this room, please?"

Sofia nodded, her heart pounding in her chest. "Okay, abuela."

Moments later, the front door erupted with a thunderous slam, signaling the departure of the mysterious intruder. Sofia's abuela cautiously opened the door and hurried downstairs, ensuring the coast was clear. Relief washed over her as she confirmed the presence was no longer within their home.

"It seems," her abuela breathed, her voice filled with fear and gratitude, "something frightened him away." Hastily, she locked the front door and double-checked that all the windows were secured.

Meanwhile, Sofia sat on the stairs, her eyes fixed on her abuela's frantic movements.

"Abuela, who was that person?" Sofia asked.

Her abuela sighed, exhaustion etched on her face. "Please, sit down; it's time you hear the truth."

Sofia plopped onto the couch next to her grandmother, her heart still racing from the encounter. "Abuela, that...that was the whistling man, wasn't it?"

Her grandmother glanced at her; she fumbled to find the right words, "The whistling man, he's this horrifying figure who roams the world carrying a sack filled with human bones."

"Ew." Sofia's face twisted in disgust.

"He's a disfigured, hunchbacked man who breaks into the homes of unsuspecting sleepers. Tonight, he chose our house. You see, he needed a quiet place to count the bones in his sack, one by one. That's the eerie noise we heard earlier. But tonight, something in our home scared him away, thank goodness."

Sofia's eyes widened in disbelief. "But where did he come from? How did he become this dreadful man?"

"He once was an ordinary boy who unfortunately witnessed his father murder his mother and, in a rage, murdered his father. His grandfather would not forgive him, so he tied the boy to a tree, whipped his back repeatedly, then put his father's bones in a sack and cursed him to walk the earth carrying the sack of bones on his back. He is unable to die and must keep moving.

Sofia shivered, and a chill ran down her spine. "That's... that's truly terrifying, abuela."

"But fear not, my dear. The whistling man is gone now, vanished into the night. There's no need to be scared anymore. I promise," her grandmother assured, her voice laced with a comforting tone.

Sofia crawled into her bed that night, her heart finally calming down, for the whistling man had vanished into the shadows. Yet, an underlying fear lingered in her fragile mind, tormenting her thoughts with the possibility of his return. Just to be sure, she cautiously inspected her window, ensuring its closure and locking it tight.

Still, unease gripped her as she pulled her curtains together, revealing a chilling sight outside her bedroom window.

A mysteriously hunched-over man prowled along the dimly lit street, a weighty sack casually draped across his bent back.

Pumpkin Party

Nancy and Jay were craving a bone-chilling tale, a story that would scare them. With a sinister twinkle in his eye, their father paused to gather his thoughts. Suspense hung heavy in the air before he finally began, "You see, kids, a bewitching secret exists beneath the cloak of every Halloween night. Between the haunted hours of 11 and midnight, skeleton parties unfold, concealed from prying eyes like ours."

Nancy's curiosity grew; she was entangled in the web of her father's words. With excitement, she inquired, "What kind of parties, Dad? I must know."

A grin stretched across their father's face as he delved deeper into the story. "Well, Nancy," he whispered, "these gatherings are unlike any you've ever imagined. From their eternal sleep, skeletons claw their way up from beneath the cold earth, emerging to relish in their limited freedom. They rise to the surface, hungry for one night of entertainment."

Jay's eyes widened in confusion, his eyes wandering the room, "They...they dance and party, Dad?" he asked, barely able to comprehend what his dad was saying.

"Yes, they do," he replied. "In the moonlit darkness, these skeletal beings shimmy and sway, bones rattling and bony fingers intertwined, dancing until they can't dance anymore. They embrace their stolen time until the fateful chime of midnight, at which point they retreat to their underground slumber, sinking back into the cold, lifeless earth they call home."

Nancy and Jay exchanged chilling glances, their minds weaving visions of ghoulish parties at pumpkin patches.

Jay let out a bursting laugh that rang through the room. "Come on, Dad. That's got to be the fakest thing I've ever heard."

His dad smiled wider, "I understand your skepticism, son. But believe me; I witnessed it with my own two eyes."

Nancy couldn't help but interject. Her eyes widened with curiosity, "You mean, you actually saw it? For real?"

He nodded, "Yes, indeed. Many moons ago, when I was just a little boy, I stumbled upon a forbidden pumpkin patch during a festival. The area was off-limits, but I couldn't resist the temptation. And there, before me, were the dancing skeletons."

"Wow!" Nancy gasped; her jaw dropped in wonder. She yearned to witness the eerie spectacle for herself. It became her sole desire for Halloween night.

And so, the following night, Nancy and Jay embarked on their annual trick-or-treating adventure. Nancy told her dad they'd be home before the clock struck eleven. However, deep down, she harbored secret plans of her own that would lead her straight into the heart of that skeleton dance.

After a long night of collecting treats, Nancy and her little brother, Jay, ventured towards the local pumpkin patch. As they stepped onto the desolate path, uncertainty filled the air, and Jay couldn't help but voice his concerns. "We're going to be in so much trouble," Jay uttered, his voice trembling with unease.

Rolling her eyes ever so slightly, Nancy reassured him, "I'll handle Mom and Dad, Jay."

Skepticism etched across his face, "You may think that now, but trust me, Nancy, Mom, and Dad will be furious that we were late."

"Jay, this is a once-in-a-lifetime opportunity to witness skeletons-dancing. You may not believe it, but I do."

Jay shrugged. "Come on, Nancy, even I'm not that gullible. You can't honestly believe his spooky story."

Once again, Nancy rolled her eyes, "Just wait and see, Jay. The truth will reveal itself in due time. Prepare yourself for bewilderment."

With a resigned shrug, Jay began to open a candy wrapper, contemplating his sister's conviction. "Alright, I'll give it a chance. But only if you inspect my candy before I eat it."

Nancy, taken aback momentarily, nodded, "Agreed."

Once number eleven flickered on Nancy's phone, followed by a series of missed calls from her father, anticipation began to build within her. A strange excitement gnawed at her core as if something extraordinary was about to unfold before her eyes - something that involved skeletons.

Unfortunately, disappointment entered their hearts as time ticked on without anything happening. Exhaustion settled on Jay's face; he wanted to go home. With every passing minute, their hopes crumbled. Her phone turned 11:13 – and they gave up. They snatched their candy bags and prepared to go home. But fate had other plans in store for them. As they walked away, their spirits weighed heavy with disappointment, and a growling sound began from behind.

It was a sound that froze them in their tracks. They slowly pivoted, eyes widening with a curiosity of equal parts fear and wonder.

Rising from the very earth emerged an unearthly spectacle - skeletons clawing their way out of their slumber. A melody abruptly cascaded through the air, its haunting notes intertwining with the gasps caught in their throats.

Nancy and Jay quickly hid, vanishing behind a bunch of hay barrels. There, they were concealed from the bony gaze of the dancing skeletons.

Their mouths dropped open, abandoned by logic and rationality, for what was happening before their eyes was a sight to see.

In that extraordinary moment, bathed in the glow of moonlight, Nancy and Jay bore witness to a spectacle that would forever rewrite the boundaries of their reality.

The Well

Cindy Jenkins found herself trapped within the hotel her mom worked in as her weary eyes witnessed her mother change linens on not one, not two, but six hotel rooms. With a heavy sigh and wandering eyes, Cindy's shoulders slumped.

Her mother looked over to see her daughter's boredom. "Why don't you take a brief break, my dear?" her mother suggested. "Go for a stroll, and stretch your legs before my shifts are over."

Jolting at the idea, Cindy treaded the endless hallway before sliding into the elevator. She descended into the courtyard.

Her gaze surveyed her surroundings, cautious yet intrigued, as she embarked on her journey.

Sharing a smile with anyone who crossed her path, Cindy's wanderings gradually guided her towards what looked like an aged, weathered well, steeped in mysteries untold. Compelled by curiosity, Cindy peered into its darkened depths, her lips curving into a grin. She grabbed a penny from her pocket; she held it tight, made a wish, and then tossed it in.

Before Cindy could turn away, a bone-chilling cry echoed from within the well, "Ouch!"

Stunned, Cindy murmured a quiet "hello" into the darkness.

A low, haunting response filled the air. "Hi."

Paralyzed in fear and a creeping sense of unease, Cindy fixed her gaze upon the bottomless well. How could anyone be down there? She mustered the courage to ask a question.

"Who... who are you?" her voice trembled.

A desperate plea emerged from the depths. "I am a lonely girl desperately wanting friendship. Will you jump into the darkness to be my friend forever?"

Cindy stepped back, her heart pounding in fear. The question rendered her speechless. She was unsure how to respond, and the voice spoke again.

"I need a friend, and that friend shall be you. Take the plunge and join me, won't you?" whispered the eerie voice, echoing through the chilling air.

Cindy trembled with terror, knowing that going down into that well, meant she'd be there forever.

Refusing to surrender herself, she mustered every ounce of courage and cried out, "No!"

Gathering her quivering legs, she sprinted frantically until she collided with her mother, who was clocking out of work for the day.

Immediately, she wrapped her arms around her mom, seeking protection.

"Are you okay?" Her mother asked.

Not wanting to tell her the truth, she simply replied, "It's nothing, Mom. I just love you, that's all."

Her mother reciprocated the embrace, "You ready to go home?"

"Yes, please."

Cindy spent that night looking through the internet, trying to figure out who that little girl in the well could be. Her heart sank as she uncovered a chilling tale. Long ago, a young girl had vanished from the hotel, her whereabouts still unknown. A chill crept up Cindy's spine. The haunting image of that girl trapped within the depths of that well bothered her; she couldn't sleep that night.

Part of Cindy wanted to return and continue their conversation, but fear held her back. Deep down, she knew that if she returned, the girl in the well would try to entice her to join her in that dark well. Cindy decided never to go back again.

As the years went by, Cindy grew older and found herself returning with her mother to work for a day. However, that haunted well never left her thoughts. Compelled by curiosity, Cindy went back to the well. She approached the edge with trembling steps and pulled out a shiny penny from her pocket.

Tossing it down the seemingly bottomless pit, Cindy eagerly awaited a response from the girl trapped within. But silence filled the air, leaving her puzzled and unsettled. She tossed another coin, hoping for some form of communication but still nothing.

Perplexed and disturbed by this disconcerting silence, Cindy tried to brush it off as mere figments of her imagination. But deep down, she couldn't shake off the feeling that something sinister lurked within the depths of that well.

She was waiting for her mom in the lobby when suddenly; a little girl burst in and breathlessly told her mom about a chilling encounter with a girl trapped in a well, talking to her! The girl's mom dismissed it as mere imagination, but Cindy knew the girl in the well was still desperately searching for a friend.

It made sense that the poor girl longed for companionship from someone her age. That's precisely why she never conversed with her when she returned to the well older. She wanted someone her age to be friends with; she was happy it was never her and hoped no child would fall for her ghostly kindness.

Ghost Bus

Maria shivered in the bitter cold as she stood at the desolate bus stop, awaiting her ride to Toluca.

Night had already fallen, and the eerie silence made her uncomfortable. But despite the late hour, she couldn't refuse her boss's urgent request to stay late at work, something she didn't want to do again. Coming off work late and waiting alone at a bus stop was scary.

As she stood there, her breath visible in the frigid air, she squinted into the distance and saw flickering lights approaching. "Finally," Maria murmured to herself, rubbing her hands together in an attempt to warm them.

The bus pulled up, and to her surprise, it appeared different from the usual one she's boarded before. A sense of unease washed over her as she noticed its worn-out appearance and the crowd of people inside.

An unsettling feeling settled in her gut when she stepped onto the bus. Handing her ticket to the driver, she was met with a dismissive wave, as if her presence meant nothing.

Looking around, she observed the passengers, frozen in place, fixated on some unseen point ahead. Only a lone seat remained, tucked away at the far end of the bus. Reluctantly, Maria took her seat, and the bus lurched forward. Something was definitely out of place. She couldn't help but study the passengers, wearing outdated clothes.

The men, the women, and even the children all exhibited an unnatural stillness, their behavior opposing the norms she encountered daily on her usual transit.

Maria peered out the window, her gaze lost in the outside world. Exhaustion tugged at her eyelids, threatening to plunge her into sleep, but she fought the urge, jolting awake each time. The thought of going to sleep aboard this peculiar vehicle scared her.

The eerie silence on the bus sent shivers down Maria's spine. An indescribable uneasiness gnawed at her stomach, urging her to escape the vehicle. Even though she was merely moments away from her destination, she couldn't ignore the overpowering need to run away. Suddenly, the bus abruptly stopped in Toluca, far from where Maria intended to disembark. Confusion swept over her as she scanned the other passengers, unsure of whom the driver was addressing.

"Get off the bus," the driver commanded in a sinister, raspy voice.

Maria's eyes darted around, searching for someone else he could be referring to. Yet, his intense gaze was directed only at her, mirrored in the rearview mirror. Trembling, she pointed to herself, ensuring he was talking to her. The driver nodded, affirming her worst fears. Gripping her bag tightly, she gingerly stood and trudged toward him, aware of the curious gazes of the other riders fixated on her.

"Por favor," Maria managed to stammer, before the driver interrupted with a stern glare.

"This is the end for you. Get off," he stated.

Powerless against his eerie authority, Maria stepped off the bus. As she turned to face the driver, he warned her, "Go now, for if you don't, you will never leave this bus."

With no other option, Maria nicely complied, embarking on a short walk to the nearest bus stop. Upon arrival, she noticed a couple waiting there, their concerned expressions reflecting her distress. Sensing their empathy, they approached her, asking about her well-being. It was then that Maria recounted the strange incident on the bus. The couple's eyes widened with fear, one blurting out, "Ghost bus!"

Confused and terrified, Maria implored for an explanation.

"You didn't look at the bus as it drove away, did you?" he asked, worry etched on his face.

Wordlessly, she shook her head. "No."

"Thank goodness," he breathed, relief washing over him.

"When you see that bus for what it truly is as it pulls away, you'll see the passengers as nothing but skeletons. That bus met its tragic demise long ago, plummeting off a mountain edge. Now, it haunts this station, picking up unsuspecting souls needing a ride to Toluca late at night. If, by chance, you were to look at the bus's departure, your life would end within a matter of days, and your very soul would forever be trapped in the seat you occupied."

Maria's jaw dropped, her mind struggling to comprehend the magnitude of what she had just heard.

"I swear, I didn't look," she assured them.

"Good, that's good," the man replied, relief evident in his voice. "We've heard countless stories from those who've seen and boarded that cursed bus. It's a stroke of luck that you never laid your eyes upon it as it left."

But what Maria hid within the recesses of her being was the truth: she had looked at the bus as it drove away.

<u>La Llorona</u>
(The Weeping Woman)

In the depths of twilight, as the sun bid farewell to the horizon, Roberto found himself engrossed in a ball game with his cousin. The minutes slipped through his fingers like grains of sand, and darkness stealthily enveloped the world around them. Yet as Roberto ventured towards his beloved Abuela's home, a mysterious sensation slithered up his spine, injecting his veins with an icy dread.

Haunted by this unsettling presence, Roberto cast anxious glances over his shoulder, desperately seeking solace in the familiar surroundings. Faint whispers of paranoia danced on the fringes of his mind, urging him to pick up his pace. He knew he wasn't alone.

At last, when his weary feet reached the threshold of Abuela's house, a screeching cry tugged at his ears.

Abuela extended her hand like an anchor without warning, seizing hold of Roberto's coat with urgency. Swiftly, she whisked him inside, ensuring he was safe.

Through the small window pane, her wise eyes scanned the world outside, etching lines of worry onto her face.

"Que paso, Abuela?" Roberto inquired, his voice trembling.

"Do you know who lurks outside?" she replied, her tone laden with concern.

Roberto shook his head, his eyes wide with curiosity and fear. "No."

His Abuela motioned him towards the living room, beckoning him to take a seat amidst a gathering of other neighborhood children. Perplexed, Roberto settled in, gazing at his Abuela for answers.

"Abuela, I don't understand," his voice quivered.

She gently touched his shoulder, guiding him closer to the center of the room. "Come, dear ones, gather here, and I shall unveil the sinister truth that demands your silence tonight."

"But I heard someone, a woman, crying," Roberto interjected, his voice laced with confusion.

"The thing you encountered was no ordinary woman," Abuela somberly uttered. "You heard the echoes of La Llorona."

"Who?" Roberto asked.

"Settle down, my children, for I shall tell you a tale that will ignite both fascination and fear within your hearts. You deserve to be forewarned about the enigma that is La Llorona." She began to speak, her voice filled with a chilling tone, "Listen closely, children, for what I am about to share is not just a mere fable. It is a dark legend, an urban myth that has been proven time and time again. The tale of La Llorona, the weeping woman, is no fabrication. It is real, and I am about to reveal the closest you will come to the truth behind this haunting apparition. Long ago, a woman named Maria resided in a humble rural village. Maria possessed an enchanting beauty that captivated the hearts of every young man who gazed upon her. Despite coming from a poverty-stricken family, her looks were renowned throughout the land. One fateful day, a wealthy businessman arrived in the village. Among all the women, Maria was the only one who bewitched his eyes. As his gaze met her radiant face, he became transfixed, unable and unwilling to tear his eyes away. Maria herself was entranced by this man, succumbing to love with each passing moment. She fell under his spell, enraptured by his charms and the fact that he loved only her.

After spending significant time together, he proposed, and she eagerly accepted, ready to embark on the next chapter of her life. They married swiftly and soon started a family, welcoming two sons into the world. Her husband's business required him to travel extensively; leaving home so frequently that little attention was spared for Maria. He doted solely on their boys, leaving her neglected and forgotten as she grew older. Then one day, he returned to the village with a younger woman at his side, bidding farewell to their sons while completely disregarding Maria. With her heart shattered, anger and vengeance consumed her. Taking her sons to the river, she drowned them in despicable revenge. But as the fog of fury lifted, she realized the immense magnitude of her actions. Frantically, she searched for her beloved children, but it was too late. The river had swallowed them, never to return. Days later, her lifeless body was discovered near the riverbank. In taking her own life, she committed the ultimate sin, now eternally trapped between the realms of the living and the dead. She earned the name La Llorona, the weeping woman, for she weeps endlessly, tormented by the loss of her children as she ceaselessly roams in search of them. That is why it is dangerous to wander the streets late at night, for she lurks in the darkness, mistaking unsuspecting souls for her long-lost sons. Her presence brings nothing but malevolence and misfortune to those unfortunate enough to encounter her."

"Abuela, what will she do if she catches one of us?" Roberto questioned, his voice trembling with fear.

His grandmother leaned in closer, her eyes filled with a mix of wisdom and dread. "She will drag you into the river, child," she whispered back, the words sending shivers down their spines. Suddenly, the sound of a woman's mournful cries pierced the air from outside. Abuela placed a finger to her lips, urging silence upon the frightened children. They held their breath, watching intently as the shadowy figure of a woman passed by their window, her sorrowful sobs barely audible. Roberto knew it had to be her, La Llorona herself. They waited in stillness until her presence faded and the haunting cries dissipated.

"That is why you must never venture outside to play or roam when darkness falls. If she catches you, no one can save you," Abuela cautioned, her voice heavy with horror.

The children sat there, their eyes locked with one another, paralyzed by fear. Roberto always listened to his wise grandmother; she possessed knowledge beyond their years.

He believed every word she spoke. Once the streets had cleared and the neighborhood children had returned to their families, Abuela tucked Roberto into bed.

"Night, my sweetheart, nothing to worry about; she's gone."

But sleep eluded him that night, as his mind was consumed by the dread that La Llorona would be waiting outside his window, ready to claim him as her own.

Genoskwa

(The Stone Giant)

Pablo raced through the woods, his chest heaving with every breath. He glanced over his shoulder repeatedly, his heart pounding with fear. How had he gotten himself into such a mess?

It all traced back to his foolish friend Jackson, a troublemaker who never considers the consequences of his actions or the safety of others.

Earlier that day, Jackson had approached Pablo with a wild idea. He claimed that a stone giant had been spotted by one of their neighbors the previous night, and he wanted Pablo to join him in hunting down this mythical creature.

Not satisfied simply with Pablo's help, Jackson had rallied the townsfolk, convincing them that this monster needed to be annihilated before it took matters into its own hands and began devouring everyone in town.

Jackson possessed a silver tongue, and it wasn't long before a group of twenty individuals had joined the cause.

Pablo didn't honestly believe in the existence of a Stone Giant, but he couldn't resist the opportunity to witness the disappointment on their faces when they realized the woods held nothing more than empty lies. However, Pablo underestimated the situation. He had underestimated just how wrong he could be.

Armed with hunting gear and flashlights, the group gathered at the edge of the woods, ready to venture into the darkness and put an end to the monster.

When Pablo approached the woods, he had a nagging feeling deep in his gut, a warning that urged him to turn around and head back home. But instead of listening to his instincts, he foolishly ignored them, marching straight into a deadly trap. At first, everything seemed normal. Jackson led the group without a hitch, and there were no eerie sounds or ominous footsteps approaching, nor any sign of the woodland creatures that inhabited the area.

That was until one man let out a blood-curdling scream. He had been standing just behind Pablo one moment, and he vanished into thin air the next. His scream faded into the distance as his lifeless body hurtled back toward the group, inducing a wave of panic and chaos.

Every single person scattered in different directions, desperately seeking an escape. But the more they ran, the louder the cries for help echoed through the night. Then, Pablo knew without a shred of doubt that something lurked within those mysterious woods - something powerful and evil, known only as the Stone Giant.

Pablo halted his frenzied sprint, gasping for air. Seeking refuge behind a sturdy oak, he struggled to suppress his labored breaths. The anguished cries reverberated through the air, the locals pleading for help as they dashed through the darkness.

Foolish, thought Pablo, to scream so loudly; they were merely signaling their location to the Stone Giant.

Taking a moment to assess his surroundings, Pablo searched for signs of his whereabouts. He needed to find his way back.

Hoping he was headed in the right direction, he resumed his desperate sprint. The screams had ceased, though Pablo couldn't tell if it was due to a newfound silence or if death had claimed them all.

He continued to flee, vigilant in his efforts to avoid the pursuing creature, constantly scanning his surroundings. Finally, a glimmer of light pierced through the inky blackness, beckoning him forward.

Surely, it must be the street, the gateway to the town's safety. Summoning every ounce of strength in his weary legs, he pressed on, refusing to succumb to exhaustion. Yet, just as hope nearly engulfed him, a voice shattered the silence - Jackson, his friend, calling out for him.

Pablo skidded to a halt, his head whipping around to locate his dear friend. Unbelievably, Jackson raced toward him, defying the odds of survival. Urging him to hurry, but time betraying their reunion, tragedy unfolded. The trees parted, revealing the Stone Giant's colossal form causing the earth to quake beneath it.

With a single, callous grasp, it claimed Jackson - snatching him into the darkened woods. Jackson's agonizing screams pierced the air, frightening Pablo.

Yet, what could he do?

Venturing after his friend would only get him killed. With a heavy heart, Pablo turned his back on the nightmare unfolding, fleeing for his safety.

He became the sole survivor, plagued by relentless nightmares, tormented by the fear of the Stone Giant's retribution – eternally haunted.

Pablo was forever altered, forever marked by the night imprinted on his soul. The memories replayed incessantly, a relentless specter of terror. He vowed never to venture into those woods again, warning others to steer clear, for it was in those depths that the Stone Giant lived.

The Cold One

Sarah struggled with her mother's constant refusal to let her go out with her friends, even if it was just to see a movie. Her overprotective mother always shut down her plans. However, Sarah had a different plan in mind – she would sneak out of her window and meet up with her friends once her mother fell asleep.

Suddenly, the doorbell interrupted Sarah's thoughts. She sat up in bed and listened as her grandmother entered. Sarah had no idea that her grandmother was coming over for dinner.

She silently hoped that her grandmother wouldn't stay too long, as she was itching to go out with her friends.

Sarah joined them for dinner but refused to speak to her mother the entire time. She continued with the silent treatment she had mastered since her mother's constant rejections.

The tension between Sarah and her mother did not go unnoticed by her grandmother, who ignored it for a while. However, as time passed, Sarah's grandmother couldn't ignore it any longer.

She entered Sarah's bedroom, sat on the edge of her bed, and inquired about what was troubling her. Sarah poured out her frustrations about her unfair mother, who never allowed her any freedom, eagerly awaiting the day she turned eighteen and could do as she pleased.

Her grandmother took a deep breath and explained why her mother had become so overprotective. She recounted a story from her youth when she had once snuck out of the house to meet up with friends, only for things to go terribly wrong.

Sarah perked up, intrigued by what her grandmother had to say. Her grandmother proceeded to tell the tale. "One evening, after dinner, she had slipped out to join her friends for a small gathering at the park. At first, everything seemed fine, but then a mysterious man appeared out of nowhere. A pale figure lurks on the park's outskirts, observing her and her friends. Your mother was the first to notice him and became uneasy. She decided to leave, listening to her intuition. Unfortunately, her friends opted to stay; not realizing the danger awaited them. The next day, they discovered they had been attacked by this man they called the cold one.

You see, Sarah, your mother had encountered what is known as a blood-sucking vampire."

Sarah scoffed at the notion of vampires, finding it ridiculous. However, her grandmother's stern expression reminded her this was no laughing matter. These creatures, known as Apotamkin or "the cold ones," had been sighted for years, lurking under the cover of darkness, searching for unsuspecting prey.

Her grandmother confided in Sarah, revealing that the events of that fateful night and her friends' fate caused her over-protectiveness.

Her grandmother continued, "She fears that if she lets you venture out into the night, you too might encounter one of these cold ones."

Sarah pondered this momentarily, realizing that whether or not vampires were real, it would be dangerous for her to sneak out and leave. Suddenly, she understood her mother's cautious nature.

An hour passed, Sarah's grandmother bid her farewell, and her mother went to bed.

Contemplating the idea of slipping out through her bedroom window to meet her friends, Sarah ultimately decided against it.

She chose to remain inside, acknowledging that maybe – just

maybe there are vampires out there, and if there were, what else exists?

I'll be right back

Caroline and her boyfriend, Greg, decided on a spur-of-the-moment camping trip to Lake Woodboard. It wasn't too far away, just in the next town, and it was something they hadn't done before.

The journey took them nearly four hours, but they believed a peaceful weekend together would be worth it. Once they arrived, Caroline began unpacking while Greg set up the tent. They looked forward to a night of relaxation under the stars, enjoying the peacefulness. Lost in each other's company, they chatted for hours, completely unaware that someone was lurking in the shadows, watching their every move.

This mysterious figure had hidden behind a tree for the past two hours, eavesdropping on their conversation.

With a smile, Greg said to Caroline, "I'll be right back." He got up and walked away.

Curious, Caroline shouted, "Where are you going?"

"I had too much to drink," he yelled back.

As Caroline rummaged through her purse, searching for chapstick to soothe her lips from the cold weather, she heard a branch snap behind her. Turning around, she peered into the dark woods, shrugging off the noise and continuing her search. Finally finding her chapstick, she was startled again by another noise behind her. Jumping to her feet, she anxiously scanned the surroundings, her fear growing. "Greg!" she called out, desperate for his presence.

But there was no response. She followed his path, searching the area. "Greg!" she called again. Suddenly, Greg emerged from the woods, catching her off guard.

"Hey!"

Startled, Caroline stumbled backward and tripped over a branch, landing on her hip. "Ow!" she let out a cry of pain.

Rushing to her side, Greg asked, "Are you okay?"

"That hurt," she replied, clearly unhappy with him.

"I'm sorry; I didn't mean to startle you. I saw something and wanted to show you."

"I called you multiple times; you could have at least answered."

"I'm sorry; I walked further than I should have."

"You think?" she retorted, her anger evident as she stood up. Shrugging off the incident, Caroline brushed herself off. "Thank goodness my leg feels okay."

"Are you alright? I'm so sorry," Greg said, expressing concern.

"I'll survive."

"Can you walk?"

"Yeah," she replied, stretching out her leg. "It feels fine."

"Come with me; I want to show you something."

Carefully navigating through the woods, making sure not to trip on any obstacles, they ventured a little further away from their campfire. Greg pointed to a tree and said, "Look at that."

Carved with a knife on the tree were the words, "I'll be back tonight!"

"What the..." Caroline exclaimed.

"Weird... right?" Greg agreed.

"Very." Caroline looked around and noticed large boot prints in the dirt leading into the woods. "Do you see that?" she asked Greg.

"I didn't notice those before. Wow."

"Maybe we should go back to our tent."

Greg chuckled. "Don't be scared now. Who knows how long this has been here?"

"Or when it was carved? It could have just happened," Caroline said.

"Alright, let's go," Greg said.

Caroline couldn't shake the uneasy feeling throughout their journey back to the campfire. Once they returned, they discovered her belongings scattered on the ground.

"My stuff!" she exclaimed, hurriedly picking them up.

Greg attempted to help, suggesting, "Maybe the wind knocked it over?"

"There's hardly any wind tonight. And would the wind really scatter all my things like this? I don't think so."

Greg knew she was upset and frightened. He regretted showing her the carving on the tree; it had been too much.

"Let's get some sleep. I'm tired," Caroline decided.

Nodding in agreement, Greg said, "Sounds good."

They let the fire burn out naturally as they cuddled up in their tent. Exhausted, Caroline tried to sleep but couldn't get the image of the tree carving out of her mind. Greg, however, paid no mind to it and quickly dozed off. Just as Caroline started drifting off, the sound of breaking branches surrounded their tent. She sat up, straining her ears as the noises transformed into the footsteps of someone walking around. Caroline nudged Greg to wake him up, persistently nudging until his eyes opened.

"Yeah," he whispered.

"Someone's out there," she whispered back.

"What?"

"Someone's out there." Startled, Greg sat up and rubbed his eyes, searching for any signs of the intruder. He gestured for Caroline to stay quiet. After a few minutes, the noises and shadows vanished.

"I'm going to check outside," he said.

"Are you crazy?" she smacked his arm.

"I won't be able to sleep unless I know for sure," he insisted.

Sighing, Caroline shook her head. "Fine, whatever."

Greg put on his shoes, grabbed a flashlight, and exited the tent, assuring

Caroline he'd be right back. He zipped up the tent and left her waiting, but he took so long that she couldn't hear a sound from outside. Worried, she put on her shoes, snatched her flashlight, and followed suit. Instead of calling out his name and alerting anyone nearby, she swept the area with her light. To her horror, she saw Greg's shoes lying on the ground. Caroline covered her mouth to stifle her scream. She searched for his other shoe and found it, along with his flashlight, smeared with blood.

Tears streamed down her face as she realized what she was looking at. She turned, the beam of light revealing the dark woods. Uncertain of what to do, she started shouting Greg's name, hoping for a response. As she called out for him, she heard a noise behind her. She spun around to see a figure standing near their tent, squinting her eyes to identify Greg's blue and white checkered shirt. Relieved, she ran over, shouting,

"Greg!" Yet, as she closed in, she realized it wasn't him.

Greg and Caroline vanished without a trace...

Out in the Cold

Marilyn Summers was completely clueless about the situation that had unfolded. Due to the relentless downpour, her car had steered off the edge of the empty road. The only logical explanation was that she had lost control, sending her crashing into a nearby tree.

Clinging onto her jacket, she shivered in the cold, drenched and desperate for help. Abandoning her car, she embarked on a quest to find any form of help. Hoping for a passing vehicle to stop for her, she walked on and on, yet no one stopped.

Just when all hope seemed lost, she heard laughter from a distance. She thought there must be something or someone ahead, relieved at the prospect of potential aid.

The rain finally stopped as she approached the source of the laughter, granting her clearer vision. Illuminated by a single light, a group of individuals hung out in a secluded area of the woods, seemingly engrossed in a lively celebration.

Marilyn approached some of the people and pleaded for help. Instead of responding to her distress, they turned around and asked her to join them.

Confused by what they were saying, she persisted in seeking their help, explaining the wreckage of her car not too far away and her urgent need for a phone to call for a tow. Yet, they seemed only interested in recruiting her into their party.

A man stepped forward, inquiring about her well-being. Though she claimed to be physically OK, just a tad chilly, he casually dismissed her concerns, suggesting that she would eventually adapt to the unforgiving coldness of the woods.

Realizing that she couldn't linger for long, Marilyn voiced her determination to have her car towed and depart swiftly, as she had a conference meeting to attend in the morning. However, his response was a mocking laugh accompanied by an unsettling remark about her fate.

Confused by his words, she struggled to comprehend their meaning. Quickly excusing herself from the bizarre encounter, she darted away, convinced that the individuals were deranged.

She fled as fast as her legs could carry her, leaving the onlookers in her wake. Finally, she caught sight of her car in the distance. As she slowed down to catch her breath, headlights appeared on the horizon. Frantically, she ran into the middle of the road, flailing her arms and screaming for help. Yet, the approaching car did not slow down; it sped up.

She desperately tried maneuvering out of its path, but it was too late. The vehicle crashed directly into her, or so it seemed. She watched with bewilderment as the car passed right through her, leaving her unharmed.

Baffled by this ghostly encounter, she peered through her car's driver's side window, only to find her lifeless body there, eyes frozen wide open. It dawned on Marilyn that she was already dead.

The Cave

Sarah glanced at Ken and Jenny and suggested, "Why don't we just set up camp in that cave we passed by earlier?"

After finally figuring out how to assemble one of the tents, Ken replied, "That actually sounds like a fun idea."

Jenny expressed her concerns, shaking her head. "I'm not sure how safe that would be."

"What do you mean? It's a cave; it seems safer than being out here," Sarah argued.

Jenny sat down with her map on a nearby rock. "This is the best spot to set up camp. Are you really suggesting we sleep in a cave?"

Sarah nodded enthusiastically, "Yeah!"

Jenny glanced at Ken, seeking his input. "And you?"

"Sounds like a fun adventure to me," Ken agreed.

Jenny had no choice but to go along with their decision. They had agreed beforehand to stick together, no matter what. No matter how much she disagreed, going off on her own would be a bad move. They gathered their belongings and moved into the nearby cave. Jenny set up her tent beside theirs, as the cave was spacious enough for both. The cave turned out to be unlike any other. Its walls were covered in ancient depictions. Jenny tried to decipher their meaning but couldn't understand. The only thing unsettled her was the images of strange creatures attacking people.

She showed them to Sarah and Ken, hoping to change their minds, but it didn't faze them. Ken gathered some wood as night fell and built a fire outside the cave.

Jenny couldn't shake off the feeling that camping there was somehow a bad idea. A few hikers passing by noticed their camp and looked on in bewilderment.

"Hi," one of the girls greeted them. They waved back, and the girl paused, engaging in a conversation. "Do you guys know anything about this cave?"

Jenny, Ken, and Sarah shook their heads.

The woman nodded and warned them, "Legend has it that anyone who sleeps in this cave gets eaten alive."

Ken and Sarah burst into laughter. "What?" Sarah continued to laugh.

The woman was shocked at their reaction. "I'm serious. Campers who mess with this cave have never been seen again. You should really consider finding another spot." She pleaded with them but eventually walked away, not caring anymore.

Jenny wasn't surprised that someone had said something. After seeing the drawings on the cave walls, she felt more concerned than the others. The more she thought about it, the more frightened she became at the possibility of being eaten alive by these strange creatures. She packed her belongings and asked them to come with her, but they refused. They couldn't believe that a stranger had affected her so much.

Sarah rolled her eyes and laughed. "You're such a scaredy cat."

Jenny shook her head. "Whatever."

"Look at her; she's scared," Ken joined in the laughter.

Jenny didn't care what they called her. She moved down the hill and returned to their original campsite.

She set up a place where she could keep an eye on them in case something happened. As hours passed, Jenny fell asleep, comforted by the sounds of nature. Camping had always been a relaxing experience, and she enjoyed it immensely. In the middle of the night, a blood-curdling scream jolted her awake.

She quickly emerged from her tent, searching for the source of the sound. Looking up towards the cave, she couldn't see anything in the darkness. She began walking towards it, screaming for Ken and Sarah, but she could only hear Sarah's frightened screams.

Jenny realized they couldn't hear her. Then, Sarah came running down the hill and collided with Jenny, causing her to fall and hurt her wrist on a nearby rock.

"Sarah, wait!" Jenny called out.

Ken was nowhere to be found. Jenny repeatedly called out for him, but there was no answer. She knew she shouldn't, but she approached the cave to investigate. She rushed back to her tent and grabbed her flashlight before cautiously approaching the cave.

From within, she could hear strange noises. She shone the light down and saw a trail of blood leading from outside into the cave. As she slowly walked towards it, she could hear a faint crunching sound. She stopped at the entrance, fearing something might grab her if she entered. She directed the flashlight inside and was horrified to see four or five tall, thin, gray creatures devouring Ken. She gasped, and they all turned towards her, their mouths revealing razor-sharp teeth. They resembled the creatures depicted on the cave walls. She knew that something was deeply wrong with this cave.

At that moment, she froze, unable to move. She attempted to run, but her legs felt paralyzed. The creatures paused their feeding and slowly crawled toward her.

Finally, summoning enough strength, she screamed in horror, turned around, and fled as fast as she could, leaving all her camping equipment behind. Never go camping again.

Hook Man

Two teenagers sat in a car near an abandoned campsite, a popular spot for teenage couples seeking privacy. Josie and her boyfriend Mike were kissing in the car. It was a special night for Mike, as his father had finally trusted him with his car. He knew he had to return it in the same pristine condition when he took it; that was no problem, he thought.

Suddenly, Josie pushed Mike away. "Did you hear something?" she asked, her voice concerned.

Mike paused, straining his ears to listen. "I don't hear anything," he replied casually.

"No, I swear I heard something," Josie insisted.

Mike grew annoyed and tried to resume their kissing. "It's just your imagination," he dismissed her worries.

Refusing to back down, Josie shoved him away. "I'm telling you, I didn't imagine it. I heard something!"

Rolling his eyes, Mike offered to investigate. "You want me to go check it out?"

Alarmed, she grabbed his arm, shaking her head vigorously. "No, are you crazy? What if there's someone out there?"

Confused, Mike looked around the deserted area. "Have you looked around? There's no one here."

Reluctantly, Josie peered out of her window, searching for any signs of intruders. "I guess you're right."

Despite Mike's reassurance, Josie couldn't shake the unsettling feeling. "I still want to leave."

Taking a deep breath, Mike finally relented. "Fine, let's go."

As Mike started the car, a loud thud echoed from the back, causing the vehicle to shake. They exchanged fearful glances, unsure of what could have caused such a disturbance.

Mike quickly sped away, fueled by his fear of the unknown. A heavy, unnerving silence consumed the rest of the journey back to Josie's house. After pulling into Josie's driveway, Mike turned off the car and offered to open her door.

Walking around the car, he froze in shock when he discovered something sticking out from the trunk. His eyes were wide with terror, and Mike covered his mouth in disbelief.

Josie, desperate to understand the cause of his distress, jumped out of the car and rushed to the back. There, dangling from the trunk was a bloody hook. Unable to contain her fear, Josie let out a piercing scream.

They both knew that if they had stayed any longer, they could have become the next victims of the mysterious hook man.

THE END

Turn the page and write your own spooky story...

Title: _________________________________

THE END

About the Author

Reyna Young resides in San Francisco, Ca with her husband John and son Logan. Together they run Last Doorway Productions, an independent film company. She is also known as TV Horror Hostess Miss Misery of Miss Misery's Movie Massacre. Director, Actress and Author of the Monsters book series which includes The Creature of Stowe Cabin, Hanover Falls, Horror Lullabies and Mr. Torture, published by Black Bed Sheet Books. She also continues publishing horror comic books through Scattered Comics.

Reyna Young's
Halloween Night
Book Series

Paperback and Ebook available on Amazon today!

Buy Book One Today!

www.lastdoorwayproductions.com